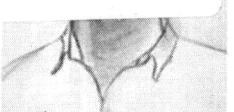

 he Gospel According to Everyone

Words Martin Wroe
Portraits Meg Wroe
Illustration, Design and Layout Rob Pepper
Photography Stefano Cagnoni

© 2011 Martin Wroe, Meg Wroe, Rob Pepper
All rights reserved. Published 2011
ISBN 978-1-4478-0973-9

'The Church is the Fifth Gospel'

How come in Church we only ever hear gospels from four men in Palestine 2,000 years ago.

What if we were to hear a reading from a Fifth Gospel, the stories of the people sitting right next to us ?

The woman who gave up her child for adoption. The gardener who notices God in the roses. The gay man shunned by his children. The atheist who found he'd become a believer.

What if we heard from The Gospel According to Everyone?

Dedication

For
Pat and Dave Tomlinson
and
Sheila and Tim Pigrem

Over many years, helping people
find their gospel truth
in an urban parish
called St Lukes,
West Holloway

he Gospel According To Everyone

The Fifth Gospel	Page 6
The Gospel According to Ivy	Page 14
The Gospel According to John	Page 20
The Gospel According to Sam	Page 28
The Gospel According to Judi	Page 32
The Gospel According to Ezekiel	Page 40
The Gospel According to Hilary	Page 46
The Gospel According to Julia	Page 52
The Gospel According to Stefano	Page 60
The Gospel According to Sissy	Page 68
The Gospel According to Agnes	Page 74
The Gospel According to Doreen	Page 78
The Gospel According to Dean	Page 84

The Fifth Gospel -
The Gospel According to Everyone

erhaps you didn't know that your neighbour gave up her child for adoption. Or that the woman you chat to waiting for the train in the morning is living with an illness that will finally take her life. Has the gay man who sits by you in church on a Sunday ever told you about his estranged wife and the grown up kids who shun him. Or the woman putting that leaflet through your letterbox? She's living on the breadline, being beaten by her partner, dreading having to return to her flat.

Everyone of us is a story but for most of us no-one else has read it. Your closest friends may not know your story. You may not know it yourself because you never had a moment to sit down and organise the material, to weave the colourful threads of your life into a narrative with compelling characters, remarkable twists and even, occasionally, some dramatic resolution.

In our increasingly populous neighbourhoods facial recognition is the closest many of us get to knowing who our neighbours are - and that's not very close. But one of the virtues in being part of a faith community is becoming friends with people unlike you. Over time you come to know women and men who are not part of your peer group, to whom you would have otherwise remained a stranger. And one day - sharing a hymn book, at the communion rail, over coffee - you catch a glimpse of their story, the one you've never heard. Another week, another glimpse.

On the island of Iona a couple of years back someone said, 'The Church is the Fifth Gospel'. I can't remember who was saying it when the phrase took hold of me but I couldn't stop wondering about it. 'The Fifth Gospel' is a phrase that's been used of the Gospel of Thomas (the one that didn't get into the Bible) and of Palestine, where the stories of the first four - Luke and John, Matthew and Mark - were told. The C20th theologian Karl Barth used the phrase of the Book of Isaiah while Rudolph

'Everyone of us is a story but for

Steiner used it for a lecture series claiming to describe previously unrecorded events in the life of Jesus. But someone wise connected this phrase to the Church, the community of people scattered through history and geography, who try to follow in the way of Jesus Christ. 'The Church is the Fifth Gospel.'

In many churches on a Sunday morning there is a reading 'according to' Matthew, Mark, Luke or John, a reading known as 'The Gospel Reading'. In some churches the reader picks up the Gospel Book from the altar, carries it back down the aisle and when she stops, everyone turns to face her as she reads from it. At the end of the parable or miracle or eccentric genealogy, she says 'This is the Gospel of our Lord,' and, depending on the height or depth of the particular church tradition, sometimes The Gospel Book is kissed. Gospels are revered in our Christian communities. They trace the stories of the people Jesus called friends, record their conversations, watch as their community is transformed beyond anyone's expectations. But what would a Gospel Reading According to the Fifth Gospel be like ? The Gospel according to *most of us no-one else has read it.'*

the Church, the Gospel according to you and me, the Gospel according to everyone. Where would you find the text? Who would be the characters and what are their lines?

Perhaps you'd find this gospel in the lives of the people who make up the faith community you have an allegiance with, those on the edges and at the back as much as those centre-stage or at the front. Those underheard as well as those overheard. Perhaps a reading from this Gospel would be from the life of someone who is part of the story that you are part of when you are part of the story of a church.

For me that would be a reading from the life of a church called St Luke's, West Holloway in North London, a sprawling urban parish of 10,000-plus souls, located between two famous prisons, Holloway and Pentonville, and sitting about a mile north of London's Kings Cross. Our family have been part of this church for nearly three decades, and known some of its people for what might as well be for ever and ever amen. But when I bumped into one of those people, Agnes, one afternoon, I realised how little we know of the story of the people we know. She was walking down our road, campaigning for her local political party. As we talked, I realised that her gospel might be a place to begin: a single mum, living in a two bed tower-block flat, often stony broke, but never in any doubt that God would look after her and her loved ones.

I visited Agnes for tea, talked with her about her life and noticed the glinting tributaries of faith illuminating her story all the way from Africa to Holloway. I wrote her story up. I wrote it in her words, but edited and organised them according to my sensibilities as a writer, judging what would get the listener interested and what would keep them listening until the end. An hour of conversation, another hour. Thousands of words, transcribed and reflected on until some kind of theme emerged. Then edited for delivery, brief enough to retain the interest of people who really don't have to be in church on a Sunday morning. A portrait in words. A snapshot of a life. Faith and hope, love and longing. A sense of divine companionship. Good

reading from the Fifth Gospel?'

news even on the days when the news was mainly bad. A gospel.

We have an endlessly accommodating vicar at St Luke's, West Holloway called Dave Tomlinson, so when I suggested the idea of us sometimes featuring a different kind of Gospel Reading in the service – one according to our local church - he went for it. On a Sunday morning we included it in the service, chose someone to read it and I wrote these words to preface it.

It has been said that the Church is the Fifth Gospel so periodically we will feature an additional Gospel reading in our services - from the Gospel of this Church, in North London.
A reading this morning from the Gospel of St Luke's, West Holloway, according to Agnes.

The Gospel of Agnes was well received and a few weeks later we followed it up with another Gospel According to St Lukes, this one the story of Sam Murphy, a retired BT engineer and, for

'Good news even on the days when the

as long as any of us can remember, our church gardener. Our readings from the Fifth Gospel caught on. As well as offering a compelling moment of storytelling in services, they've also become an effective way of revealing our hidden lives to each other, promoting understanding and friendship. When our reading from the Fifth Gospel is followed by one from the first four it's striking to notice how those prodigals, foreigners, farmers and housewives are not so dissimilar from the charismatic characters in our indigenous gospel accounts.

Meg, my wife, is a painter and has created portraits of the subjects. Six of the originals are oil paintings and six are charcoal drawings. We are still writing and painting different people, delivering a new gospel every couple of months. Maybe there will be a second volume.

Perhaps this book could be more than a local memento for people in our urban parish. Maybe it could inspire people in other communities to create their own indigenous gospels, revealing their untold stories. We're surrounded by a great cloud of witnesses says a writer whose letter is recorded towards the end of the Bible. But most of the time we fail to witness these witnesses, fail to listen as they reveal their rich and deep and moving stories. They come from everywhere and have arrived in the same place as us, a community of faith, travelling along in the hope of a sign of grace, a snapshot of the divine. When we stop to listen, we find traces of the good news in all our stories, signs of a gospel in everyone one of us. A gospel according to everyone. A Fifth Gospel.

Martin Wroe, July 2011

The Gospel According to Ivy

thel, my sister, was born in 1927 and I was born in 1920. We lived at number 29 Ashburton Grove, where the Arsenal Stadium is now, that's where we grew up.

Dad was a brass turner, working in Holborn. He was strict but loving. Mum was marvellous. We played out on the streets as children, made our own entertainment. They called us street waifs. It was so lovely that we used to cry when they called you in, when it was getting dark and the lamplighter came along.

Some roads we weren't allowed on, like Queensland Road. There were fights up there, people drank too much. I'm not saying we didn't go there though, now and again. It still makes me sad thinking that the Stadium is now where our home is, where our street was.

From as early as I can remember we went to Sunday School at the Albany Mission on Albany

Place. It was run by the Smiths, three brothers and a sister. The oldest son was a missionary and it was exciting when he came back from Africa because he showed us his slides on the Magic Lantern. Lancelot, another of the brothers, would walk along the streets collecting children for Sunday School. I can picture him now, holding hands with the children on his way. You couldn't do that today.

Drinking was a problem in those days and we used to go to the Band of Hope where they used to pray and were against drinking. You had to say a pledge. I don't know what's happened to my pledge card. I signed it. But I must admit, I do like a nice glass of wine.

In those days people used to have to get all dressed up for church, to wear a hat and gloves. The men wore bowler hats and suits. All very refined. But in the war people stopped going so much. During the war you'd come home from work and go straight down the air raid shelter at the bottom of the garden. You stayed all night until the all clear. In our shelter it was Mum, Dad, Bob our brother and us two. Sometimes

> *did make you wonder how he could allow this.'*

Dad would go to the house to get a cup of tea. Some people died doing that - a direct hit when they were boiling the kettle. Sometimes people would say to you, 'Guess what? So and so's been killed.'

You can't just blame God for the war but it did make you wonder how he could allow this. No-one has an answer for these tragedies. Life is all ifs and whys isn't it ? Like our neighbour yesterday: two men broke into his flat and stole £7,000 from him. Why does this happen ?

We've been coming to St Luke's regularly for about five years now. Ethel's daughter Carol was married here 28 years ago and Gary her son was in the Sunday School and used to say 'Come and see me performing.' When we did we felt guilty that we didn't go to Church so we started coming again. Gary and Carol still come now, even though they've moved to Hertfordshire. That's why they're late every week. It's the friendliness we like. Church used to be just a service and then you shook hands with the vicar at the door.

'It's the friendliness we like - Church used to be just

Ethel used to play piano and loves listening to Justin. She says, 'I could sit and listen to him all day, that's my favourite thing, he's marvellous.' Dave and Pat are so friendly. Atmosphere has a lot to do with a good church. Years ago a child crying in a service would be disastrous but we love seeing the children running around. And we like the coffee.

I can walk down my street every day for a week and not see anyone to talk to but we come to church and people don't stop talking to you. Sometimes there's so many we don't even talk to Carol. We just wave at her.

It makes us feel a lot better when we come to church. We've both lost our husbands – Eric, who was married to Ethel in 1950 - and Bill who married me in 1945.

'If I'm dusting a picture of my husband,' Ethel says, 'I'll talk to him. I just say, 'It's a nice day and I wish you were here.'

I always say 'Good Morning' to Bill and 'Good Night'. After he died there was a star out there *a service and then you shook hands with the vicar.'*

over those houses, one that didn't seem to move. I was telling Judi at church about it after he died, that I thought it was Bill looking down. She said it most likely was. After a while it disappeared and she said, 'It's because he knows you're alright.'

As you get older you begin to accept dying more. As Ethel says, 'You can't live for ever can you?' I think there's a heaven up there. My Bill always believed in life after death and the church gives you confidence.

The Gospel According to John

Once, a few years ago, completely by accident, I met my granddaughter. I should never have met her and it never happened again but just for a moment we looked at each other for the first and only time. We were completely speechless.

I've never met any of my other seven grandchildren or my two great-grandchildren. My family won't allow me to see them. I've barely seen my three sons or my daughter in nearly thirty years. It's not that surprising: I raised my children to believe that someone like me is just not acceptable. So they don't accept me.

In our family we're Salvation Army, that's how I was raised, that's how I met my wife. My father was a bandsman, played the trombone, and my parents raised me as a Junior Soldier. I never

'We raised our children as good Salvationists

knew any other way of being a Christian and I loved it: the music, the meetings, the whole way of life. I learnt to play brass when I was 11, cornet, then tenor, then baritone, then bass, then trombone. I still play them all. It was no surprise to anyone that after National Service in 1956, I swapped one Army for another. I had the call to serve as an Officer, what other churches would call a minister or priest, and as a young Lieutenant I headed to Elland in Yorkshire, to lead a congregation of 20 Salvationists.

Your life is mapped out for you in the Army and it was inevitable I'd meet a woman, another officer, that we'd marry and share ministry together. And so I met and married Shena. We were posted to Ilfracombe in Devon, where our usual congregation of 30 became 120 in the summer, when elderly Salvationists came down on their holidays. Every evening we had open-air meetings, two on Saturday, three on Sunday. I played the concertina and preached, while one of us stood with the flag, and people with collection boxes were on both sides of the road.

> *but things were not all they seemed to be.'*

That was our life. We raised our four children as good Salvationists too but behind the scenes things were not all they seemed to be. Even at school I'd known my feelings were for boys rather than girls but I'd assumed this was normal. As a Salvationist sex was never talked about - your knowledge came from behind the bicycle sheds - but as an adult I became sure I was gay. And, as a married Salvation Army Officer, it meant I became involved in a double life. At first my wife had no idea but eventually my excuses for coming home late wore thin and she began to realise I was not, shall we say, being straight with her.

I can't say I was happy with myself but I was trapped in a terrible world of guilt, deception and confusion. For years I was in a cycle of beating myself up, of tears, of repentance… before the cycle started again. Finally, one day in 1982, I was outed. I received an urgent summons to the Divisional Commander's office where he read out a statement made about me and asked if it was true. I had to say 'Yes'. He demanded my resignation on the spot.

'I began to realise I was not strange but

In my late-forties, married, with four children, suddenly I had lost my job, my career and my house. My wife had to resign as well. It was one of the most traumatic experiences of my life but, as Mike, my partner, says: 'Even though the Army decided to dispense with your services, God did not.'

Being good Salvationists, my wife and children wanted me to overcome my 'problem' and I understood their view. It was, after all, the view of the Salvationism we all shared. I'd unwittingly raised my children to despise the person I'd turned out to be. They thought my being gay was some kind of compulsion whereas I have realised that it was, and is, who I am. In the end they didn't like me being around and my wife asked for a divorce.

Although I'd never felt rejected by God I'd long felt I was falling short as a Christian until one weekend I went to a conference of something called the Gay Christian Movement. It was a revelation to meet these people - Baptists, Methodists, Anglicans, evangelicals - talking about Jesus, about being gay, with no *that God was happy with my identity.'*

condemnation from anyone. I began to realise I was not strange or weird but that God was happy with my identity. Previously I didn't think God was pleased to see me but now I realised he was saying, 'Welcome John!' And slowly I began to stop living a lie.

I wrote to my family to say I'd accepted myself as both a Christian and a gay man. My oldest son, now a Salvation Officer himself, replied that I was no longer his father and that I was not going to visit him and give his children AIDS. He asked me not to contact him again.

There is a lot of ignorance in the Church, so many people carry so much prejudice, resentment and lack of forgiveness. As the years have passed I've never stopped hoping and praying the family might change their minds. They believe I have to change but as Mike and I often say, 'If tears, repentance and prayers could have changed us we would not be together now.'

The family stay in touch with my twin sister so I do pick up news. The other day I noticed an old photo of me at her house that I didn't remember. 'That's not you,' she said. 'That's your son.' It was only his slip-on shoes, which I would never wear, that convinced me it wasn't me.

The meeting with my granddaughter came at a Salvation Army Conference where I mentioned to a Scandinavian officer that my son lived there. He had no idea and to my shock he said, 'I've brought his daughter with me.' And there she was. For a moment I looked into the eyes of my own granddaughter, both of us lost for words. I've no idea what she'd been told about me but there was no reaction from the family afterwards.

My widowed sister recently married again, to a very old friend of mine but it was my son who gave her away. I wasn't invited to the wedding because she wanted my children and grandchildren there. If I had come, they would not have. Even after all these years, it can still hurt. I remember one morning, at St Luke's, watching a visiting grandfather taking his granddaughter up to receive communion and I *very old friend of mine but I wasn't invited.'*

thought of my own grandchildren and suddenly I broke down in tears. I couldn't stop sobbing.

Mike says I've committed the sin of the 'h-word' – honesty. But I don't carry any bitterness towards the family or towards the Salvation Army. I try and pray for them all. I'm probably at the top of my son's prayer list and he's at the top of mine so the Lord will sort it out one day.

Even on my deathbed I'd love to see the children and the grandchildren, just once, that is my desire, I'd love to see them. But it's all in God's hands.

The Gospel According to Sam

'd say I've been part of this church since about 1980, so that would be near enough thirty years. I started coming along after I moved to the Clocktower Estate and never really stopped.

It was nearly 20 years before that, in 1962, when I came across to London from Ireland. I grew up in County Carlow but I'd been working as a gardener in Bray and then in Dublin. I was getting about £3 a week. You can get that much for an hour these days. A relative introduced me to this posh Irish man who had a landscape gardening firm in London. I met him on the Friday and I was on the boat on the Monday. The money was better, £9 a week, and better still when I got a job in Regents Park. That was £13 a week and I worked there for four years, looking after the rose gardens.

'Sometimes I just like to look at the

I've always loved the gardening but there was so little money in it and eventually I got some classes to learn to be an electrician and that's how I ended up working for the Post Office, all over the City of London.

My Gran was a real Bible reader, who prayed a lot, but for me it wasn't until my twenties that faith came to mean something deeper, when I understood about Jesus dying and about how we're forgiven. When I first came to St Luke's, there was a Deaconess, Patsy, living in the vicarage while Tim, the vicar, lived up near me in the flat above St Francis on North Road. Then there was only a handful of us in services, we used to start the hymns with a tape-recorder. Tim organized a day to work in the garden and I said that I'd do this area over by the front wall. He looked at me with a smile and said, 'You can do more if you like!' I did end up doing more. I've been doing it ever since. I just like looking after the gardens, I enjoy it.

To me, being close to nature, can be like being close to God, like in the best gardens you have this serene state, this peaceful state. I remember

roses and marvel at them.'

when I first when to Iona, I heard it described as a thin place, where the distance between earth and heaven is not much. A few times I've been in the garden of St Luke's and felt it is also a thin place. Sometimes people want to pray in the church: one woman, who couldn't speak English, would only go as far as the doorway, no further – she just stood there. And I asked God to grant her whatever she was praying for.

We used to have a Bible Study and we had home groups. Why they petered out I don't know. We used to sit and debate, although that got a bit iffy sometimes if you ask me.

If this church wasn't here I'd miss it. It's like someone who's been married for thirty years, you might have some arguments but if they were gone you'd miss them. I like being with the earth and watching God send the sun and the rain and then seeing how everything grows. Sometimes I just like to look at the roses and marvel at them.

The Gospel According To Judi

y son will be 35 this year and it will be 35 years since I've seen him. After he was born in November 1976 I gave him up for adoption. His loss is one of many losses in my life and I've come to understand that loss doesn't go away. Loss is always with you.

There was a relationship which could have developed but the father had to go back to Canada where he already had a family. For a Christian woman, a Sunday School teacher, in an English village, to be pregnant with no husband was not ideal but the local priest and his wife were very supportive, much more than my mother. They found me a place to live while I was pregnant and when I gave birth my brother came to visit at the hospital. Everyone

'I've come to understand that loss

assumed he was my husband and thought I was just like them.

I couldn't raise the child on my own because I'd have had no support: frankly my family were dysfunctional. They didn't know what to do with children - they could be judgmental and unkind - and anyway I really wanted the boy to have a family with a dad, unlike my family where dad was often not around.

I'm an Essex girl originally, born in the 1940's, but we moved around because my father was in RAF Bomber Command. He could be away for months, and my mother, although she was deaf, ruled the roost. She wasn't what you would call motherly but she was always in charge - whether at home or at the local church. My sense of God was not quite the same as hers: I remember telling her that I saw God caring for the earth by sprinkling it with a big watering can. She was shocked, this was not her image of the divine at all.

doesn't go away, it is always with you.'

At ten I was confirmed and soon afterwards was teaching in Sunday School - we have a teaching gene in our family and a lot of my professional life has been in education, often primary children or those with special needs.

Having moved to London I became a Special Needs Teacher in a Catholic School near Euston where the Irish Catholic children would tell me there were no good Protestants. 'What about me?' I asked. 'Oh, you're fine!' they said. I learned to build bridges between communities here and took those lessons to St Luke's School in Old Street where there was a big Bengali community. I'd go home with pupils and meet Bengali mothers, terribly isolated in their flats, facing hostility and racism when they ventured out. However poor they were, they always fed me.

It was when I was doing supply teaching and I was attacked in class that my life began to take a new course. A girl said something nasty to another child about his family and he went for

> *'I knew my Bible, that life has times of*

her. He was only about eight but seemed intent on killing her. As I tried to prevent this he stood up and sent me flying. I hit my head on the table, came down on my back, and passed out. When I came to, everywhere was silent. I have never been in a more silent classroom.

In my memory this attack and the back pain that I still experience are part of a sequence of events through which my health inexorably declined. My father, a great support to me, died suddenly. An intimidating ex-prisoner moved into a flat in our house. Arthritis began to assert itself. I was mugged on Caledonian Road and then again on Cardoza Road. Previously I'd been the person to intervene in disputes - I remember stopping two men on a train from stubbing cigarette buts out on another man - but now I was withdrawing. I was changing as a person.

I became more and more unwell and if you're afraid and unhappy your physical illness gets worse. I got to the stage where I couldn't go out *darkness, that God is in the darkness...'*

through the front door. I became focussed on protecting myself so I went into isolation which is not good, psychologically or physically.

But I knew my Bible, that life has times of darkness, that God is in the darkness and eventually I went off to a Christian hospital where they help people with fatigue and burnout. A friend told me that I must find a church. That was when I walked around to the next street, and rang the doorbell of St Luke's Vicarage and there was Scott, then the vicar. Becoming part of St Luke's has played a huge role in slowly regaining my health and confidence - coming to this place, day in and day out, to meet with a small group of people and pray. I'm a different person now.

The pathway back has also involved Autogenic Therapy, a form of self-hypnosis in which you address different parts of your body by name and tell them they are ok, allowing the body to heal itself.

'I still weep some days and usually in November,

Meeting people with disabilities through Islington Disability Network and becoming active in the Circle 33 Housing Trust, I've discovered I have resources which can empower others.

Fifteen years ago I could be weepy quite often. I was facing all those feelings that had been repressed in the working years, facing all that loss – loss of health, loss of work, loss of income. Loss never goes away, especially the loss of a son and not knowing where he is, which is a cause of great grief. And coming into St Luke's, where there are lots of little boys growing up in happy families, it still catches my throat and makes me fairly weepy.

I suppose I've lived a messy life but I think the cross of Jesus is quite messy and it is the church which mistakenly tries to sanitize it. From this messy life I've found inner understanding, compassion and humility. Living on benefits can mean you face financial poverty, but I feel very rich as part of this church.

on the birthday of the son I don't know.'

My birthday is the feast of St Michael and All Angels and I always say that I've needed all the angels all the time in my life… to get out of the scrapes I've got into.

I like to mother people, to listen, to care for them, I think it's the maternal instinct that I began but was not able to complete. But I still weep some days and usually on November 5th, the birthday of the son I don't know. Our losses are always with us but the book of Isaiah says 'Comfort ye, comfort ye my people' and I find that St Luke's is a comfort to me.

The Gospel According to Ezekiel

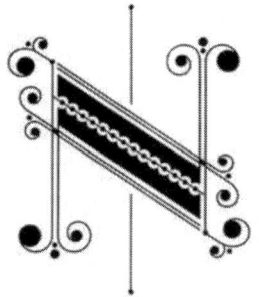

ot many people at St Luke's can say they used to work at Salisbury Cathedral. I did. I was an ordained preacher there…. Just kidding! But I did work there. I'll tell you about it.

I was born in Finsbury Park in 1961 and grew up in Surr Street, where my mum and dad lived. I went to Pools Park Primary and Sunday School at St Marks Church, Tollington Park. After Holloway Boys secondary, my first jobs were in a garage, spraying cars, sweeping out, doing a bit of mechanics. Renee used to live near us, that's how I got to know her and her sons. Later on, when she was getting old, I used to bring Renee to St Luke's in her wheelchair. She used to sit by Cissy and Doreen.

When my mum and dad retired to Jamaica I took on the flat in Surr Street but later the

'I got on to the M4 and just kept walking.

bailiffs came and took my stuff and I lost the flat. That's when I started being homeless. I only had the clothes I stood up in, a few books, some diaries that my mum had kept. I used to stay with Fred, and one time he was talking about the Summer Solstice at Stonehenge. It sounded interesting and as I had nothing to do I thought I'd walk there. Fred told me the directions. So I started walking. It was a way of seeing the world I suppose!

I walked from York Way to Notting Hill but I got double bubble delay there, I got lost, going round in circles, so I walked back to Holloway. Fred told me the directions again. I walked back to Notting Hill and this time I managed to get out from that maze and from there to Chiswick and from there I managed to get on to the M4 and I just kept walking. Down the motorway.

It took about three days walking. The police never stopped me. At night I would sleep on the grass bank at the side of the road. 'Cus of my garage background, I enjoyed watching the

Down the motorway.'

Aston Martins, the Bentleys, the Jaguars.

When I got to Stonehenge there was a big protest going on, fighting with the police about who owned the monument. People thought they shouldn't be restricted from being with the stones. I took the side of the police. I could see the stones were being damaged. Even though I've done a bit of property damage myself in the past, I don't agree with it!

Someone told me that Stonehenge was a kind of cathedral once and I ended up walking to Salisbury to see the actual cathedral. That's how I arrived in Salisbury.

I slept in pub doorways, in the graveyard, in the cathedral grounds. I started helping as a volunteer in the cathedral - labouring, moving stones, taking messages, that sort of thing. I would wander into the cathedral to listen to the service - to hear the choir singing or people saying their prayers - then I would leap back

> *'Sometimes I pray for God. If I was in*

outside in case I was needed for any jobs. In the end they took me on. I was earning £130 a week. I was still sleeping rough. I came back to London sometimes. Once the police did stop me. I was so knackered I was starting to walk onto the motorway itself! So they stopped and gave me a lift.

In the end I came back to London. I was still homeless but eventually I got my own place. Even though God is generous and will always give to you, I don't like taking advantage of people.

I've lived in Chalk Farm and in Kilburn, on Camden Road and on Cally Road. I've been coming to St Luke's for about 20 years. My faith means everything to me. I try to pray for others and for people who are ill and for people who have looked after me. Sometimes I pray for God… if I was in God's position I could never do what He does!

> *God's position I could never do what He does.'*

I might go to the Methodist Church on Cally Road before coming to St Luke's. They have the same readings: like if it's Isaiah there, it will be Isaiah here. Sometimes I go home after the service and open my Bible and read the passage again to see what I think about it.

As I get older I learn things and take steps forward. And I'm very proud of the time I worked at Salisbury Cathedral. Although my name is Ezekiel I'm not Ezekiel from the Bible. He was a prophet and I've never made a profit.

The Gospel According to Hilary

 was born and raised in Muswell Hill where my family was dysfunctional. My dad imported metals from Africa. My mother bought lots of bottles of gin. Dad was 'away quite a lot' - that's a euphemism - and high up in the Freemasons, dressing up and that kind of thing. Later he had a breakdown. It wasn't the ideal place to be a child and I escaped to the local Anglican church. I think I was trying to find a reliable family.

That was St James's in Muswell Hill, they welcomed me, but by 15 I'd decided to become a Baptist. Then I tried out the Catholics, I loved the smells and bells. My faith was like magic, everything was a sign, telling you what to do. At 17 I was 'born again' but then I went to university and people told me I had to be 'baptized in the spirit' and speak in tongues. So I did that too. I loved it because it was so right

'We spoke in other tongues but the Brethren

brain, about what you experience and feel, not all in your head.

I was a post-grad in Cambridge and I met a guy smuggling Bibles into Eastern Europe so I became God's smuggler too. I was followed into Czechoslovakia, one time, and nearly arrested. I met this guy who confided in me that he was in love with this woman. I confided in him that I was also in love with a guy. It turned out we were not in love with these people but with each other. Dave was from the Brethren and going to be a missionary so I became a missionary too. This was the early '70's, we learned Italian and went to save the Italians from Catholicism. And anything else they needed saving from. As well as Italian, we also spoke in other tongues but the Brethren didn't believe in this and kicked us out so we joined a Pentecostal missionary group.

Mum had died and when Dad became ill we came back to nurse him. Instead of going to a church we decided to get a church to come to us. We started our own, in Dad's house, on Grove Avenue in Muswell Hill. It was one of the best things I've ever been part of, more than *didn't believe in this and kicked us out.'*

sixty of us - singing, expressing the gifts of the spirit, reading the Bible, trying to share our lives. When it split in two, which is what often happens to house churches, it was so painful that I think that's when I started to lose my religion.

We put our energies into the family, into work and into politics – like running the local CND stall. I was teaching challenging kids in school and we were both training as psychotherapists. Dave says he was an agnostic, I think I was an atheist. I still used to pray in tongues though, it was a catharsis when times were tough. And I tried to strike the odd bargain with God, even though I didn't believe in him. In my head I was an atheist but maybe not in my heart.

One of our children was going right off the rails and we were at our wits end and it was only when he went along to this very evangelical Anglican church, where they were so welcoming and non-judgemental, that his life was completely transformed. That experience opened a door for me, reminded me what church can be, at its best.

'I tried to strike the odd bargain with

Still I was pretty horrified when Dave said this guy we'd known in the house church movement had become a vicar in Holloway. He came back from an evening service there and told me it had been like a meditation and the vicar, Dave Tomlinson, had no shoes on. Sounded appalling but, sulkily, I was persuaded to go along to St Luke's.

And sometimes in the music and liturgy, in the communion especially, I sensed God's presence. Sometimes I even wanted to raise my hands and had to look around and remind myself that they don't do that. I could see people on a journey together which made me realise I had to do some reflective work myself. I didn't have a theology any more: the old stuff didn't fit, but I had nothing to replace it with.

I'm still working out what I discard from a life story full of faith and church and spiritual passion. And what I don't have to discard. My faith is completely different now. Less about magic, more about symbolism. Now it integrates things that have always meant a lot to me – social awareness, the sacramental. One thing

> *God, even though I didn't believe in him.'*

I've kept is that the Body of Christ, the church, has always been about relationships for me – with potential to heal itself, or destroy itself, if the immune system breaks down. My Gospel now is about healthy reciprocal relationships, about lack of pressure, about the permission to question.

At lots of points in my life I felt I had got it, that I had arrived. But I don't feel that any more. Now it's all about walking on with others, discarding some things, discovering new things.

The Gospel According to Julia

as it operation three or operation four? Sometimes I lose track, there's been a few. Strange as it may seem it was an operation that cleared a path back to faith for me. A particularly difficult operation when it looked as if I was going to die and yet one where I became acutely conscious of a certain strength within, something on another level altogether. It's hard to describe it except to say that it was a sense that transforms, intensifies and clarifies everything.

When I was well enough I asked to see the hospital chaplain who gave me communion. It was a step on a journey back towards faith. The imagery of the body and blood in the Eucharist is especially powerful when you or others around you are suffering. Receiving communion was like an acceptance into church or faith or some bigger community. It made a link, it told me there was someone or something there for me and somehow made it physical.

My parents were not churchgoers but they sent me to Sunday School and then to schools with a Christian ethos. My mother had a strong spiritual sense, caring about community and fighting on behalf of other people. My father backed her up in writing letters. I guess I was C of E if anything - it's what you sort of absorb - but this loose connection faded. When my mother became ill and shortly after, died, this link disappeared.

I went home to live with my father and looking back I see how my mothers death completely stopped me in my tracks in any spiritual search. I couldn't equate it with faith of any kind. I tried church a couple of times but I couldn't do it: saying the Lord's Prayer would just make me cry. For about fifteen years I couldn't participate in any formal, spiritual way.

Work was busy: from being a rep for a brick company - how I met John, my partner, an

> *Eucharist is powerful when you are suffering.'*

architect - to editing magazines and children's fiction, then into gardening, editing Ground Force Magazine and working for the Diana Memorial Fund. At first I didn't take it seriously when I began having digestive problems. But the tests showed I had a tumour. I needed a major operation to remove part of my intestines.

I recovered and went back to work but was ill again seven years later. This time they diagnosed a rare form of cancer and there was a second operation. I nearly pegged it.

Through these and other operations and their recovery periods I began to look back at my – and my mother's - life again. She'd worked for the NHS and I began to sense I could do something with my experiences of being ill. That's when a job came up in PALS, the Patients Advice and Liason Service, which advises patients and tries to change the system from the inside. Having been quite ill frees you to talk to anyone about anything and it means patients know you have been there too.

'The experience of illness has offered

But there was also a change happening to me inside. In one operation, when we thought I would die, I'd been at the very bottom but somehow I'd found this strength, I'd found something else, something in me, deep inside, something core and central. It was connected to my mother who did so much for me but also to people all around trying to help, from the doctors and nurses to cleaners opening and closing windows, to family and friends. Somehow all of these things together created a certainty, a sureness that despite everything… all will be well.

So for me the experience of illness has offered a kind of transformation. It makes me think of a phoenix burned and transformed by fire. Reborn. In being treated with chemotherapy you are heated, it is like burning, like you are in the fires. But when you come out you are transformed. You see things differently.

> *transformation, you see things differently.'*

I think of it like being in a hall of mirrors at a fairground, you see doors reflected in a mirror which go on for eternity. And this experience tells me that it's possible to open any of these doors, that what we see and experience now is just one aspect of existence, that there is so much more going on.

In daily life, when things are difficult or going wrong this gives you another perspective. For example in my work with the NHS, I see how much every little thing that people do - from friends or family to the staff or even random acts of kindness from people you don't know - make such a difference in how you feel and how you respond to treatment. As you get better this clarity seems to retreat a little into the background and I'm desperate not to lose it. You could call it a closeness to God.

After taking communion I went looking for a church and ended up going to a very inclusive one in Stamford Hill led by an extraordinary woman who did healing and talked to spirits. There were only about ten of us on a busy

'I have known moments of sureness that

Sunday but it was my way back in to Christian community.

Eventually I found my way to St Luke's and was struck by a sense of community which I've come to value. John's a confirmed atheist but says I'm a nicer person when I go to church. I guess church should be good for your health, should be good for everything.

On our travels we've come across many gods in different countries and over time I've come to see how everything is linked, in all faiths, that it's all part of the whole. We discover all these differences yet something universal connects them.

Of course I have fears at some points and it's not easy. After this recent operation for example, I wouldn't be speaking like this when I was lying in bed in week four or five of treatment. I wouldn't be able to speak at all. At those times it's hard to see any further than just keeping *are on a level deeper than I can put in words.'*

going till the next moment. You focus on surviving. But I don't lose this belief in love, this is what keeps you going, the love of those around you, the love of The Other. Each time we struggle I believe we can find a new beginning, a better understanding.

At some stage I will die of this condition, like the phoenix I will be burned one time too many. But I have learned that it is where you are now in yourself that counts. And I have known moments of sureness that are on a level deeper than I can put in words. I have come to feel that death is not simply death. That disasters aren't only disasters but a place to start finding a way. That all our difficult experiences are just a starting point for something bigger and greater, a way of understanding about other people and other things. A way of understanding about God.

The Gospel According to Stef

When I first came to this church I didn't believe in God but sometime, over nearly two decades here, I started calling myself a Christian.

I grew up in a working-class and atheist household in Clerkenwell. We never went to the big church over the road. Queenie, my nan, was lapsed Irish Catholic, while Helen, my mum, was an atheist for political reasons and that's how she raised me. She still finds it hard to believe we're part of a church although she respects the strength of this community - community is at the heart of her politics. Politics, in particular socialism, is second nature to me - even as a child I sensed the injustice and unfairness in the world.

My dad split up from my mum when I was about five and as mum had to go out to work, my sister and I were mainly raised by Queenie, along with her daughter and five sons, my uncles, who were often in the house. They were

> *'I wanted to believe in a God but I couldn't because*

like fathers to me although, compared to my own father, not long over from Italy, their lives were like chalk and cheese. Four of my uncles had been in prison for theft and violence.

Sometimes it could be hard to work out where to get your values from: for instance mum taught me to resolve differences with other children through talking and not by fighting but I remember, when I was six or seven, coming home crying after a kid hit me and one of my uncles chased me straight back out of the house. He said he'd hit me himself if I didn't go back and thump the kid. I'd never run so fast in my life! As well as all this, I was the cockney kid called Stefano Cagnoni - small wonder sometimes I felt as though I didn't quite fit, didn't quite belong.

My dad was busy becoming a renowned photojournalist and when we occasionally saw him he regaled us with stories of wars and fighting and starving children. I'd been the first grammar school boy in the family and first to go to university - politics at York - and afterwards I also went into photojournalism.

of the bad things that happened to so many people.'

The early eighties were an extraordinary time to be involved in politics with the Falklands War, the Anti-Apartheid Movement, the Miners Strike and Margaret Thatcher attacking the working classes and trying to break the unions. On Saturday nights I'd put my shin pads on to dodge the copper's boots at Wapping and I'd still be wearing them next morning, playing football at Hackney Marshes.

Bernadette and I had fallen in love at University and back in London we moved in together. Leaving the Angel for a flat in Holloway felt like moving to the suburbs but we didn't know that it was one step of many on the way to church. It was one Christmas morning, after Rosa and Tom had come along, that the doors of St Luke's began to open for us. We'd woken to unwrap the presents when Bernadette had a kind of epiphany. Knee-deep in ripped wrapping paper, she felt the number of toys and 'stuff' they'd been given seemed obscene. Having had a religious upbringing - another lapsed Catholic - she felt Christmas was more than this. Needing to redress the balance, she walked over the road and into St Luke's. She was so impressed by the Service and the community that she dashed home again, picked up Rosa and whisked her back to share the experience.

After that you couldn't keep her away, she took both kids along while I stayed home and meditated on The Observer. (After Wapping, I'd taken a religious vow never to read The Times). But a dilemma arose on the Sundays when her shifts at the BBC meant she couldn't make church. The kids still wanted to go so she told them to ask the atheist in the house, but I didn't believe in going to church.

Not long after we'd first met, I wrote Bernadette a letter - we used to write letters in those days - explaining that I wanted to believe in a God but I couldn't because of the bad things that happened to so many people. Humanity's problems would be solved by people not by some invisible Being. But now, faced with my own kids wanting to go to church, I realized it wouldn't be right to force my atheism on them - and maybe understanding Christianity might help them understand their own history and *atheist and the next I wasn't.'*

society. I started taking them to church myself.

They'd go to crèche or Sunday school and I'd sit in the service. I didn't sing the hymns or take communion but as I talked to people I realised they weren't all evangelical or tub-thumping. Surprisingly, the sermons were quite interesting and I liked the fact that lots of people were up front - leading the service or saying the prayers or even sometimes preaching. It was a slightly irreverent, unpredictable community which reminded me a little of the big, unruly family I'd grown up in and after a while I actually wanted to go to church myself rather than just to take the kids.

It wasn't that one week I was an atheist and the next I wasn't but gradually I started to feel St Luke's was my home too and so I started to go up and receive communion. I'm even happy to lead the prayers sometimes - something my younger self would have found about as likely as me giving up Arsenal to support Spurs.

Like all families, St Luke's isn't perfect. Over the years there have been some fallings out. I've

'After Wapping, I'd taken a religious

upset some people. Once, ages ago, I even came close to hitting someone... but then I remembered I was in Church. Just as well as he's one of my best friends now.

I feel we're lucky to have found St Luke's and all it stands for - acceptance, community, doubt, faith. If this church was gone, I'm not sure north London would still be this wonderful place that it can be. I never before felt that I quite belonged but in this church I finally feel like I've found a home. Only this time, it's not a home I have to run from.

There's a verse in the Bible, the Book of Proverbs I'm told, which reads, 'Where there is no vision the people perish.' Politically I'm still very committed but a lot of modern politics seems to have lost a sense of vision, whereas on a good day the Church retains a vision for tackling injustice in society. Ironically it's party politics that gets stuck in concepts and creeds but when you're part of a faith community you treat people as individuals.

Even before I was a Christian, because of my

vow never to read The Times.'

work, I knew about things like the Church Urban Fund and saw the impact of the Church in impoverished areas, one of the few groups still working in places everyone else had pulled out of. At its best the Church retains a vision for the kind of stuff you find in the Bible, giving succour to those who need assistance, help to those who need support. That's why I believe so much in the winter night shelter for homeless people that our church helps organise. I wish we could do more things like that.

Christianity is socialist at heart for me, I see the gospel as about social and political change. People working together for the common good; not individuals just looking out for themselves. But had I lived opposite any other church I suspect I would not have made this journey to being a Christian.

The Gospel According to Sissy

veryone knows me as Sis or Sissy but actually my name is Florence. That's what I sign to at the bank. My brothers thought there were too many Florence's in the family so, being their sister, they called me Sis and it stuck.

There's another thing very few people know about me: I helped create the wallpaper for Prince Charles's bedroom when he was a baby.

Let me start at the beginning, which for me was 1930, when I was born in Marsden Street in Kentish Town. My dad, George, was a foreman in a pencil factory and my mum, Rebecca, was a domestic help. I was the youngest in a family of two sisters and four brothers and until I was four all eight of us lived in two rooms and a scullery. But my childhood was mainly happy. I can still see myself as a little girl running over Parliament Hill Fields with a bottle of lemonade and a spinning top and my skipping rope.

'You didn't really believe church people

My father was a drunken who used to beat my mother up. It's horrible to say but when I was seven or eight I wished him dead. Mum worked from noon till night to keep us all and I don't know why she didn't walk out on us. Then one Friday, payday, Dad came home drunk and started on mum. Luckily my brother was in and now that he was a teenager he was bigger than Dad. He told him he'd had enough of how he was treating mum and he knocked him out there and then. I think Dad never hit mum again. He was a bit more dubious after that.

We often went to church when I was young, to Sunday School in Lady Margaret Road, or to the Mission Hall in Falkland Road, where you got a cup of cocoa with a slice of bread and marg. With the War we were evacuated to the country and my Sunday School teacher used to write to me. I became very fond of her but when I came home I found out she'd been killed in an air raid. With her being so young and a church person it really shook me. I suppose you didn't really believe church people got killed like that or churches got bombed. For thirty or so years after that I never went to church, but of course I was looking after my mum who was diabetic and *got killed like that or churches got bombed'*

raising the children.

I loved embroidery and I won the school needlework prize and a scholarship to grammar school. But mum couldn't afford to let me stay on at school so I started work at the True Form shoe shop in Kentish Town. For 40 hours a week I earned £1 and they kept back four pence for my stamps.

Later I was a stenciller in John Lyons Wallpaper Factory. That's when it was announced the Queen was having a baby and when I was chosen to do the wallpaper for Prince Charles bedroom. One was a seasidescape - beachballs, shells, sand, that kind of thing – and the other was a woodscape with all kinds of trees. I never actually saw the wallpaper when it was hung and I don't know if it was for Buckingham Palace or Windsor Castle. But they did ask me to the showroom in Tottenham Court Road to see if it needed touching up. It was fine. I got a good bonus that year, 1947.

I married Bill and in 1954 Elaine was born. Next came Dawn, then Jacquie, then Carole and finally Tracy. Five daughters. Maybe it's no

'I've always liked churches, I think

surprise I never came back to church until the mid-1970's. Some of the girls wanted to join the choir… I think because they used to get half a crown to sing at weddings.

There were not many of us at St Luke's in the 1970's, we used to meet upstairs with some gas heaters to keep us warm. I volunteered to become the church cleaner so I'd pick up the girls after school and they'd play the piano while I did the cleaning. We used to have pews with a long red carpet running down the middle. If you lifted it up, you'd find beetles and cockroaches. I tried not to lift it up.

I've always believed in God and I've always liked churches, I think they give me peace of mind. My husband wasn't a believer - he said, 'seeing is believing'. But he never stopped me coming to church.

On Sundays I sit with Ivy and Doreen, us three old codgers, down the front. I love the hymns and hearing the organ. I don't like the piano… it shouldn't really be part of church although I don't think Justin will be pleased to hear me say *they give me peace of mind.'*

that. I love the choir, such beautiful music. I love the garden outside too. Bill died eight years ago but when it's his birthday I always give Sam some money for bulbs. Better to have them at St Luke's than up at the cemetery.

What gives me joy is my daughters and my five grandchildren, two boys, three girls. And I always thank God that I can still get about. I've been walking up these four flights of stairs to this flat, overlooking the Camden Road, for 48 years now. Sometimes I think a ground floor place would be nice.

I say my prayers every day, for the family, for peace in the world, for an end to war. I'm not afraid of dying and I think it's because of my faith. It's no good being afraid. Everyone goes eventually and I think your soul comes back. Jesus died and came back again and I think we do somehow.

When I walk into the church I always look up at that lovely stained glass window at the far end and I can see Jesus there and I feel as if I'm part of him.

The Gospel According To Agnes

I think of the polo mint when I think of my lowest moments. For several months a few years back I was so poor that some days all I had to eat was a polo mint. This was after my husband had left me. Our marriage had gone wrong, he had started hitting me, battering me. I remember being on the floor and calling out to him, 'Please, take your bags and leave us…'

My name is Agnes, by the way, and I have been part of St Luke's since the 1980's. My husband did leave us but that meant we became very poor. I was raising the children on my own and the money ran out. We were living in this flat, here, high up, looking over Holloway. Two beds. The girls share that room, I sleep with my teenage son in this room.

Sometimes my sister would invite us around for a meal. She said I was better off without him

'Even when I was surviving on a polo mint

but I didn't tell her we had no food on the table. The children could eat at school, but some days I didn't eat at all.

I would come to St Luke's but I would not tell anyone what was happening because I thought it was going to get better. God had always looked after me, ever since I was a child in Africa at the missionary school. I came to England when I was 19 because my family was approached by another family for me to marry their son who was well off. On the wedding day his Auntie intervened and we had to postpone the service. I was very upset.

He went home and I stayed here. I began to train in catering where I met another man who told me I should marry for love not for money. I fell pregnant with his child. After my baby was born I became depressed, but Rev Pigrem, the priest of St Luke's, would come and visit me. We would have tea and he would pray for me. That gave me strength.

I was planning on going home to marry the man who thought he was the father of my child, but

> *a day, I never stopped believing in God.'*

a school friend came to London. 'There is no need to go home,' he said. 'Stay here with me.' He wanted to marry me but first he said we should have a child to make sure we could have a family. We had two children, and we lived in a flat near St Luke's. I came to church regularly and for many years I helped in the crèche and Sunday School. The church has always meant so much to me.

I had to raise the children on my own and with God's help I have. My eldest daughter finished her degree and now has a good job. My second is doing her degree and my youngest is getting very good reports. I myself finished my degree which meant I could get a better job and things have got easier.

When I come to St Luke's I see many friends. Whatever the trouble life brings, with God all things are possible, no-one can hurt you or harm you. Seek first the kingdom of God and all these things will be added to you, this was the motto of my family. You know even when I was surviving on a polo mint a day, I never stopped believing in God. *(Given the nature of this story we agreed with 'Agnes' not to use her real name or image.)*

The Gospel According To Doreen

Whenever I hear of someone getting married at St Luke's my mind goes back over fifty years to a freezing cold Boxing Day morning in 1958. It seems like yesterday and I can see myself in my wedding dress walking through those same big old oak doors and down the aisle between the rows and rows of wooden pews towards Vicar Lea who was waiting at the front.

I was born in 1936 but I don't tell many people my age because people think I'm younger than I am and I like to keep it that way. I was brought up during the war in Beaconsfield Buildings in between the Caledonian Road and York Way, the second of seven children. We were sent along to the Paget Christian Church, just down the Cally Road from where Iceland is. It's still there. I belonged to the church club where we did singing and dancing and we used to go to

> *'My friends know I'm someone who prays,*

services on Sundays.

Dad worked at Mount Pleasant Post Office and mum looked after us. When I was 15 we moved to No 30 Penn Road but that house isn't there now, it got knocked down to make way for a road into the estate. I met my husband at a bus-stop, when I was 18. He asked me out to the pictures on Tufnell Park Road, the one that's the Odeon now. He was a builder and later went into lift engineering.

After getting married at St Luke's, what with having three children and us both having to work, I drifted away from church and my husband wasn't a church person anyway.

At first I worked in a factory for John Dickinson, the envelope people, but later I became a residential care assistant looking after the elderly, bathing them, feeding them, changing them. I always wanted to be a nurse and in residential care you're a bit like a nurse. I've always liked helping people and I still do voluntary work at Shopmobility in Wood Green five or six days a week. There's not many customers but it keeps *so they ask me to say a prayer for them'*

me active and if I sat here in the flat all day I'd be bored out of my brain.

I've never been out of England, except on a day trip once to France. My kids say, 'Come abroad on the plane with us' but I'm happy going to Butlins in Bognor Regis every year. The kids can't believe I still do it but I love Butlins, all the entertainment, near the beach and you haven't got to fly there. Just get the coach from Victoria.

Once the kids had grown up I used to go along to St Mark's Church in Tollington Park but I often wondered what had become of the church where I got married. So one Sunday morning, about twelve years ago, I came back through those doors again and into St Luke's and I've been there ever since.

When I walk into the church I feel at peace. I feel that God is present. I sit with Sissy, Ivy and Ethel, although Ethel can't be with us very often any more. We're like the older citizens of the

'By remembering people you've lost it

church. I try to get there about a quarter past ten to get a place on the front row and then I keep it for the others. Actually, I also get there early because I like to hear Justin and the choir practising.

My friends know I'm someone who prays, so they ask me to say a prayer for them sometimes like my friends wife got ill and he asked me to pray for her. I've got my Bible here in the flat and I read that. My faith means a lot to me. If I'm on a train or a bus I'll often pray, under my breath, I'll pray: 'Take us all safe… and the driver.' Especially if you're on a train and it stops half way, I'll say 'Please God let the train move again.'

I've booked for my funeral. I want the service at St Luke's and I've put down Dave to do it. I've chosen my hymns - Abide With Me, The Old Rugged Cross and Amazing Grace - and when we're all on the way out I want Elvis Presley singing You Saw Me Crying in the Chapel.

keeps them alive in your mind.'

My kids tell me I'm morbid, to have planned it all but I'm not worried about death. Losing two of my brothers made me decide to plan it. I believe there is life after death but how do we know because no-one we know of has ever come back have they?

I like the All Saints service we do every year, when we remember people who've died. I remember my mum and dad and my two brothers and three friends who've died. I write down all their names so they can be read out in the service. By remembering people you've lost it keeps them alive in your mind....

The Gospel According To Dean

I started cycling on New Year's Day 1994, at Cape Agulhas, the southernmost tip of Africa, where the Indian and the Atlantic Oceans meet. First I cycled up the west coast of South Africa, before reaching the long, dry roads of Namibia, then briefly into Botswana and Zimbabwe before pushing on into Zambia and the bush, the real Africa. At night I would make camp with small groups of people, farmers, or I would pitch my tent in the bush. Sometimes I'd sleep under the stars, as long as I could stop mosquitoes or Army Ants from attacking me.

I'd finished studying and many of my contemporaries were heading to Europe or North America. But I'd always had a strong affinity with the landscape. I felt like I was an African, I wanted to embrace Africa, to escape the claustrophopia of the apartheid years and

'Sometimes they would offer me a

see what South Africa looked like from the rest of Africa. I had my tent, sleeping bag, clothes and a short-wave radio. My plan was to cycle all the way up through the continent, a route which would take me nearly 10,000 miles to Tunisia.

I love cycling, it creates special connections. People would invite me to their house for food or to sleep. Sometimes they would offer me a woman to comfort me through the night. I declined these very kind offers but it reminded me of Bible stories where missionaries lived by faith, not knowing each morning where they would sleep that night. I was 24 years old, from an evangelical Christian church and involved with a missionary organisation called YWAM. On my tape-recorder, I'd listen to the music of this American singer Keith Green. Maybe I'd even end up cycling to his home in Texas, a kind of pilgrimage.

I cycled on and on. Most days it was an extraordinary feeling. A thousand miles of mystery to your left, a thousand miles of the unknown to your right. People would ask, 'Where are you going?' and I'd answer, 'I'm

> *woman to comfort me through the night.'*

going North.' And that answer was enough.

I became aware of the economic poverty of people in comparison to my life but also that there was a lot of happiness. There was tragedy and death - many mothers had lost a child, AIDS was real - but people also lived far more fulfilled lives than you'd guess from the image of Africans portrayed in the western media.

I looked rough, very rough. I looked like someone who was living off the land. A lot of the time I was in survival mode. Some days I wanted to give up. I felt I was at the very edges of life. Living was very simple, just getting some food, travelling and connecting with people. I was physically and emotionally sustained by my spiritual health. I felt like every minute of the journey I was celebrating the presence of God in the mystery of creation – feeling, hearing, seeing, smelling – that every sense was working and I was often overwhelmed.

By the time I got to Nairobi in Kenya I was completely broke and much the worse for wear. Luckily I bumped into a South African diplomat

'Every minute of the journey I was celebrating

who invited me to stay at her house and that led to a job selling satellite dishes. I needed some money before I could carry on cycling. But I got held up a bit longer. The genocide had begun in Rwanda and 600,000 people had fled over the border into Tanzania, creating a humanitarian crisis. I found myself in charge of logistics for a sprawling refugee camp run by the United Nations High Commission For Refugees, co-ordinating supplies from Nairobi to the Rwandan border.

I still planned to get back on the bike but when I was on a break from the refugee camp I met this lovely woman called Emma, who worked at the British Council in Nairobi. She held me up a bit longer. Then the UN transferred me to Lokichocio on the border of southern Sudan where I had to organise small planes to be loaded with 17 tons of grain. We flew them to places where local people, trapped by conflict, had marked the ground, and we dropped the grain from the sky. Food which would keep them alive.

the presence of God in the mystery of creation .'

Eventually, I got on my bike again. I cycled on to Uganda. Soon I was in the volcanic mountains of what used to be called Zaire, then into the Congo, and then Gabon where the roads were poor, tropical rain storms would stop everything and sometimes the only food was monkey-meat. I was glad to stop and worship with different Christian communities. Some were very evangelical and some very Catholic and most were mixed up with ancient African folk religion. I joined in with this great cacophony of religion.

Religion in Africa is not an exact science, but coming from a conservative evangelical church, the journey was giving me a new outlook. I started to realise that a lot of the time religion is just about the flies buzzing on the surface of things but that the real stuff is deep underneath.

By now it was 1996, two years since I'd set off and I was meandering. By the time I reached Togo I was concerned about whether I could get to Tunisia. The Sahara Desert was in my way. I was used to drinking river water and eating from the forest but few people crossed the Sahara alone and survived. I cycled the coast road to Ghana, then to Cote d'Ivoire and caught a train to Burkina Faso. By the time I got to Bamoko in Mali my journey was coming to an end.

I never made it to Tunisia, nor went on to Texas to pay homage to Keith Green, but I remember a song of his I used to sing a lot, from Psalm 51: 'Create in me a clean heart O God, renew a right spirit within me.' And looking back from where I am now in mid-life - running a business, paying the bills, raising children - that trip did give me a new kind of heart. And strangely, finding St Luke's, was also part of that journey: a community which recognises that we're part of something bigger, that we don't have all the answers, that we can be content with not knowing, that we don't know where the journey will take us. I found so many good things when I cycled through Africa but probably the most important was the one I wasn't looking for. I found Emma, who became my wife.

THE SKY'S WINDOW
by Martin Wroe

Finding the mysterious in the mundane, the sacramental in the ordinary, these 'lines and lyrics in search of a numinous now' offer a fresh perspective on life from first beginnings to final endings. All try to offer a sideways glance, a fleeting glimpse, of the unseen Love behind all things. Exploring the ordinary 'with a hunch that it contains more than itself', with the hope that a prayer can become a poem and a poem can be read like prayer.

www.lulu.com/product/paperback/the-skys-window/414281

ELEMENTAL
by Martin Wroe, Malcolm Doney, Rob Pepper

Earth. Water. Air. Fire The stuff that matters. In a series of extended meditations, Malcolm Doney and Martin Wroe explore each of the four elements as a way of asking who we are, what we're made of ... and why we're here. The stuff of life. Earth. Water. Air. Fire With illustrations by Rob Pepper.

www.lulu.com/product/paperback/elemental/6084126

CAN YOU HEAR THE MUSIC?
by Cole Moreton, Mark Halliday, Martin Wroe

Three writers offer words in search of wonders. The author Cole Moreton, the poet Mark Halliday and the journalist Martin Wroe collaborate on a collection of poems that are full of honesty, doubt and beauty.

www.lulu.com/product/paperback/can-you-hear-the-music/1449875

To see more artwork by Rob Pepper visit
www.robpepper.co.uk

To see more art by Meg Wroe visit
www.megwroe.co.uk

Printed in Great Britain
by Amazon.co.uk, Ltd.,
Marston Gate.